T0127512

vodka cocktails

Over 50 classic mixes for every occasion,
shown in 100 stunning photographs

Stuart Walton

LORENZ BOOKS

Contents

Introduction

In one sense, vodka is the closest thing to perfection ever conceived in the history of spirits. Had it been invented in the era of alcopops and ice beers, it would have been hailed as a supremely adept piece of marketing wizardry. Nobody, other than a confirmed teetotaller, could possibly dislike it, for the simple reason that it tastes of nothing whatsoever. It is pure, unadulterated, uncomplicated alcohol. At least, most of it is.

When serving vodka, everything should be almost painfully cold to the touch. The bottle should be kept in the freezer and the glasses should also be iced. If there isn't a heavy mist of condensation on the outside of the glass, it isn't cold enough. Some vodka shots are thrown back like schnapps, owing to an old folk belief that if you inhale the fumes for more than a split second, you will get too drunk too quickly. The aged vodkas, and specialities such as Zubrowka, are more often sipped slowly and appreciatively. A little shot glass is traditional, but in some homes a rather larger, narrow tumbler, or even something like a goblet wine glass, is used. Cold vodka is the classic accompaniment to Russian caviar, itself served on heaps of ice. In the Scandinavian countries, it is drunk, like aquavit, with marinated and smoked fish such as herring, mackerel and even salmon.

Many of the modern cocktails are based on the principle of blending a range of different, often exotic fruit flavours over a vodka base that doesn't interfere with the taste of them. This book includes all the vodka favourites from the classic era, cocktails based on today's ultra-fashionable flavoured vodkas, and a tempting array of vodka drinks that are shaken or stirred with other spirits, mixers, juices, fresh fruits and even ice cream. The following pages are a taster's tour of the best ones. Try them wisely, and have fun.

Right: You don't have to go skiing to chill out with an ice cold vodka cocktail such as this Après-Ski.

What is vodka?

The word "vodka" is a Russian endearment meaning "little water", from their word for water, *voda*. That in turn derives from the widespread European practice of referring to all distillates originally as a form of water (as in *aqua vitae* or *eau de vie*).

Precisely because it is such a simple drink, it is almost impossible to pinpoint the origins of vodka. A potent spirit distilled from various grains has been made in Poland, Russia and the Baltic states since the very early days of distillation in Europe. But as to where a drink specifically recognizable as vodka first arose is a matter for the Poles and the Russians to sort out between themselves. (Most outsiders now tend to come down on the Polish side.) What

Right: This smooth Stolichnaya vodka should be sipped appreciatively.

is certain is that, by the time home distillation had become a favoured way of passing the long winters in Poland, peasant families were producing their own domestic vodkas extensively.

Vodka is still very much the drink of gastronomic choice in its native lands, drunk as aperitif, digestif and even as an accompaniment to food. It is nearly always taken icy-cold, preceded in Polish homes by the ritual wishing of good health – *na zdrowie* – to one's family and friends. The quantities consumed may raise eyebrows in our Western unit-counting culture, but a vodka hangover is very rare, owing to the purity of the drink.

Flavoured vodka

Perhaps the most celebrated flavoured product is Zubrowka – bison-grass vodka – which is generally sold with a blade of grass in the bottle,

Above: Blue label Absolut (left) is unflavoured, while Absolut Citron (right) has a musky lemony tinge.

bison grass being the gourmet preference of the wild bison that roam the forests of eastern Poland.

Other flavoured vodkas include Wisniowka (cherries), Limonnaya (lemon) and the Swedish Absolut company's Kurant (blackcurrant), all of which are appetizing drinks. Pieprzowka is infused with chilli peppers, and has a burning, spicy finish. Russia's Okhotnichya – "Hunter's Vodka" – is impregnated with orange rind, ginger root, coffee beans, juniper berries and even a drop of white port.

Neutral vodka

Unflavoured vodkas are produced all over the world now, although most grades are only intended to

Below: Smirnoff, with its basic red label (left), is the market leader in vodka. Blue label (right) is a higher-strength version.

be served in mixed drinks. Russian Stolichnaya, particularly the Cristall bottling, is an honourable, silky-smooth exception. Smirnoff makes three types, in red, blue and black labels to denote varying strength. Scandinavian vodkas such as Finlandia and Absolut have their deserved followings, while most British vodka tends to be little more than patent alcohol. Also seen on the export markets is Polish Pure Spirit, bottled at around 70% ABV.

How vodka is made

Although potatoes and other vegetables have been used to make vodka at various times in its history, nowadays it is made virtually exclusively from grains, principally rye. A basic mash is made by malting the grains, and encouraging them to ferment with cultured yeasts. The resulting brew is then continuously distilled in a column still to increasing degrees of alcoholic strength, driving off nearly all of the higher alcohols.

As a final insurance against flavour, the spirit is filtered through a layer of charcoal, which strips it of any remaining character. It is then bottled at an average of 37.5% ABV.

Above: This Pieprzowka vodka (left) has been coloured and flavoured with chillies. Cherry vodka (right) has a lustrous, deep red colour and is intensely fruity.

In the case of flavoured vodkas, the aromatizing elements are added to the new spirit after rectification, and left to infuse over long periods – sometimes as long as three years or more. Occasionally, a speciality vodka will be aged in cask and take on a tinge of colour; others derive their exotic hues from spices, flowers or nuts.

Cocktail equipment

To make a successful bartender, you will need a few essential pieces of equipment. The most vital and flamboyant is the cocktail shaker, but what you can find in the kitchen can usually stand in for the rest.

Cocktail shaker

The shaker is used for drinks that need good mixing but don't have to be crystal-clear. Once the ingredients have been thoroughly amalgamated in the presence of ice, the temperature clouds up the drink. Cocktail shakers are usually made of stainless steel, but can also be silver, hard plastic or tough glass. The Boston shaker is made of two cup-type containers that fit over each other, one normally made of glass, the other of metal. This type is often preferred by professional bartenders. For beginners, the classic three-piece shaker is easier to handle, with its base to hold the ice and liquids, a top fitted with a built-in strainer and a tight-fitting cap. Make sure you hold on to that cap while you are shaking. As a rough rule, the drink is ready when the shaker has become almost too painfully cold to hold, which is generally not more than around 15–20 seconds.

Measure or "jigger"

Cocktail shakers usually come with a standard measure – known in American parlance as a "jigger" – for apportioning out the ingredients. This is usually a single-piece double cup, with one side a whole measure

Above: Measuring jug and spoons

and the other a half. Once you have established the capacity of the two sides, you will save a great deal of bother.

Measuring jug and spoons

If you don't have a jigger, you can use a jug and/or a set of spoons for measuring out the required quantities. The measurements can be in single (25ml/1fl oz) or double (50ml/2fl oz) bar measures. Do not switch from one type of measurement to another within the same recipe.

Above: Measure or "jigger"

Left: Cocktail shaker

Blender or liquidizer

Goblet blenders are the best shape for mixing cocktails that need to be aerated, as well as for creating frothy cocktails or ones made with finely crushed ice. Attempting to break up whole ice cubes in the blender may very well blunt the blades. Opt for an ice bag or dish towel, a rolling pin and plenty of brute force, or better still, use an ice crusher.

Ice bags

These plastic bags that can be filled with water and frozen are a kind of disposable ice tray. You simply press each piece of ice out of them, tearing through the plastic as you go. They also have the advantage of making more rounded pieces of ice, as opposed to the hard-angled cubes that some ice trays produce.

Ice crusher

If the prospect of breaking up ice with a hammer and dish towel comes to seem almost as much of a penance as working on a chain gang, an ice-crushing machine is the answer. It comes in two parts. You fill the top with whole ice cubes, put the lid on and, while

Below: Wooden hammer and towel

pressing down on the top, turn the gramophone-type handle on the side. Take the top half off to retrieve the crystals of ice "snow" from the lower part. Crushed ice is used to fill the glasses for drinks that are to be served frappé. It naturally melts very quickly, though, compared to cubes.

Wooden hammer

Use a wooden hammer for crushing ice. The end of a wooden rolling pin works just as well.

Towel or ice bag

A towel or bag is essential for holding ice cubes when crushing, whether you are creating roughly cracked lumps or a fine snow. It must be scrupulously clean.

Ice bucket and chiller bucket

An ice bucket is useful if you are going to be making several cocktails in quick succession. They are not completely hermetic though, and ice will eventually melt in them, albeit a little more slowly than if left at room temperature. It should not be confused with a chiller bucket for bottles of champagne and white wine, which is bigger and has handles on the sides, but doesn't have a lid. A chiller bucket is intended to be filled with iced water, as opposed to ice alone.

Below: Ice crusher

Mixing pitcher or bar glass

It is useful to have a container in which to mix and stir drinks that are not shaken. The pitcher or bar glass should be large enough to hold two or three drinks. This vessel is intended for drinks that are meant to be clear, not cloudy.

Bar spoon

These long-handled spoons can reach to the bottom of the tallest tumblers and are used in jugs, or for mixing the drink directly in the glass. Some varieties of bar spoon

Above: Bar spoon, muddlers and corkscrew

Left: Mixing pitcher

look like a large swizzle-stick, with a long spiral-shaped handle and a disc at one end.

Muddler

A long stick with a bulbous end, the muddler is used for crushing sugar or mint leaves, and so is particularly useful when creating juleps or smashes. A variety of sizes is available. It should be used like a pestle in a mixing jug; the smaller version is for use in an individual glass. At a pinch, a flattish spoon can be used instead

of a muddler, but then you will find it more awkward to apply sideways rather than downward pressure when trying to press those mint leaves.

Strainer

Used for pouring drinks from a shaker or mixing jug into a cocktail glass, the strainer's function is to remove the ice with which the drink has been prepared. Some drinks are served with the ice in (or "on the rocks") but most aren't, the reason being that you don't want the ice to unhelpfully dilute the drink. The best strainer, known professionally as a Hawthorn strainer, is made from stainless steel and looks like a flat spoon with holes and a curl of wire on the underside. It is held over the top of the glass to keep the ice and any other solid ingredients back.

Corkscrew

The fold-up type of corkscrew is known as the Waiter's Friend, and incorporates a can opener and bottle-top flipper as well as the screw itself. It is the most useful version to have to hand as it suits all purposes. The spin-handled corkscrew with a blade for cutting foil is the best one for opening fine wines.

Above: Nutmeg grater, zester and canelle knife

Sharp knife and squeezer

Citrus fruit is essential in countless cocktails. A good quality, sharp knife is required for halving the fruit, and the squeezer for extracting its juice. Although fruit juice presses are quicker to use, they are more expensive and more boring to wash up afterwards.

Nutmeg grater

A tiny grater with small holes, for grating nutmeg over egg-nogs, frothy and creamy drinks. If this sounds too fiddly, buy ready-ground nutmeg instead.

Zester and canelle knife

These are used for presenting fruit attractively to garnish glasses. If you don't already have them, don't feel obliged to run out and buy them, since drinks can look equally attractive with simply sliced fruit. The zester has a row of tiny holes that remove the top layer of skin off a citrus fruit when dragged across it (although the finest gauge on your multi-purpose grater was also designed for just this job).

A canelle knife (from the French word for a "channel" or "groove") is for making decorative stripes in the skins of a whole fruit. When sliced, they then have a groovy-looking serrated edge. It is, in effect, a narrow-gauged version of a traditional potato peeler, but is purely for decorative purposes.

Egg whisk

Use a whisk to beat a little frothy texture into egg white before you add it to the shaker. It helps the texture of the finished drink no end. An ordinary balloon whisk will do the trick, although for culinary uses, a rotary whisk with a handle (or the electric specimen) is best.

Right: Cocktail sticks and swizzle-sticks

Cocktail sticks and swizzle-sticks

Cocktail sticks are mainly decorative, used for holding ingredients such as olives that would otherwise sink to the bottom of the glass. And if you intend to eat the olive, it's handier if it's already speared, so that you don't have to commit the appalling faux pas of dipping a finger into the drink to catch it. A swizzle-stick is useful for stirring a drink, and may be substituted by food items such as a stick of celery in a Bloody Mary.

Glasses

To ensure that glasses are sparkling clean, they should always be washed and dried with a glass cloth. Although some recipes suggest chilled glasses, don't put best crystal in the freezer; leave it at the back of the refrigerator instead. An hour should be enough.

Collins glass

The tallest of the tumblers, narrow with perfectly straight sides, a Collins glass holds about 350ml/

Left: Collins glass

12fl oz, and is usually used for serving long drinks made with fresh juices or finished with a sparkling mixer such as soda. This glass can also stand in as the highball glass, which is traditionally slightly less tall. Uses: Dickson's Bloody Mary, Kempinsky Fizz, and all drinks that are to be "topped up" with anything.

Cocktail glass or Martini glass

This elegant glass is a wide conical bowl on a tall stem: a design that keeps cocktails cool by keeping warm hands away from the drink. It is by far the most widely used glass, so a set is essential. The design belies the fact that the capacity of this glass is relatively small (about three standard measures). Uses: The classic Martini and its variations, and almost any short, sharp, strong cocktail, including creamy ones.

Left: Cocktail glass or Martini glass

Above: Tumbler or rocks glass and liqueur glass

Tumbler or rocks glass

Classic, short whisky tumblers are used for shorter drinks, served on the rocks, and generally for drinks that are stirred rather than shaken. They should hold about 250ml/8fl oz. Uses: Screwdriver, Black Russian, Piranha and Cooch Behar.

Liqueur glass

Tiny liqueur glasses were traditionally used to serve small measures of unmixed drinks, and hold no more than 80ml/3fl oz. Uses: Straight vodka, served ice cold.

Above: Champagne flute

Champagne flute

This is the more acceptable glass to use for quality sparkling drinks. It is more efficient at conserving the bubbles since there is less surface area for them to break on. Always choose one with good depth, as the shorter ones look too parsimonious. Uses: Kir Lethale and Vodka and Kumquat Lemonade.

Large cocktail goblet

Available in various sizes and shapes, large cocktail goblets are good for serving larger frothy

Left: Large cocktail goblet

drinks, or drinks containing puréed fruit or coconut cream. The wider rim of this type of glass leaves plenty of room for flamboyant and colourful decorations. Uses: Katinka, Soft Fruit and Ginger Cup, Pushkin's Punch and SOS.

Shot glass

A tiny glass with a capacity of no more than 50ml/2fl oz, the shot glass is used for those very short, lethally strong cocktails known as shooters. If you're going to make a shooter, this is absolutely the only glass to use. No substitute will be accepted. The glass itself is usually extremely thick, as these drinks are intended to be thrown back in one, and then the glass slammed down fairly peremptorily on the bar counter. Uses: Straight vodka. Go for it.

Right: Shot glass

Tricks of the trade

It is worth mastering the techniques for the preparation of good-looking drinks. The following pages give you precise directions for some of the essential procedures, such as crushing ice, as well as some not-so-essential skills, such as making decorative ice cubes. Learning these tricks of the trade is what will distinguish the dedicated bartender from the amateur dabbler.

Crushing ice

Some cocktails require cracked or crushed ice for adding to glasses, or a finely crushed ice "snow" for blending. It isn't a good idea to break ice up in a blender or food processor as you may find it damages the blades. Instead:

1 Lay out a cloth, such as a clean glass cloth or dish towel, on a work surface, and cover half of it with ice cubes. (If you wish, you can also use a cloth ice bag.)

2 Fold the cloth over and, using a rolling pin or mallet, smash down on the ice firmly several times, until you achieve the required fineness.

3 Spoon the ice into glasses or a pitcher. Fine ice snow must be used immediately because it melts, but cracked or roughly crushed ice can be stored in the freezer in plastic bags.

Bartending know-how
For a moderate-sized social gathering, you may have to stay up all night with a sledgehammer. Alternatively, just buy an ice crusher.

Shaking cocktails

Cocktails that contain sugar syrups or creams require more than just a stir; they are combined and chilled with a brief shake. Remember that it is possible to shake only one or two servings at once, so you may have to work quickly in batches. Always use fresh ice each time.

1 Add four or five ice cubes to the shaker and pour in all the ingredients.

2 Put the lid on the shaker. Hold the shaker firmly in one hand, keeping the lid in place with the other hand.

3 Shake vigorously for about 15 seconds to blend simple concoctions, and for 20–30 seconds for drinks with sugar syrups or cream. The shaker should feel extremely cold.

4 Remove the small cap and pour into the prepared glass, using a strainer if the shaker is not already fitted with one.

Bartending know-how
Never shake anything sparkling. This will flatten it.

Making decorative ice cubes

These can instantly jolly up the simplest of cocktails. Flavour and colour the water with fruit juices or bitters, and freeze in three stages.

1 Half-fill each compartment of an ice cube tray with water and place in the freezer for 2–3 hours.

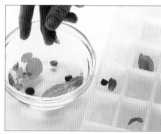

2 Prepare the fruit, olives, mint leaves, lemon rind, raisins or borage flowers and dip each briefly in water. Place in the ice-cube trays, put in the freezer and freeze again.

3 Top up the ice-cube trays with water and return to the freezer to freeze completely. Use as required, but only in one drink at each session.

Frosting glasses

The appearance and taste of a cocktail are enhanced if the rim of your glass is frosted. After frosting, place the glass in the refrigerator to chill until needed.

1 Hold the glass upside down, so the juice does not run down the glass. Rub the rim with the cut surface of a lemon, lime, orange or even a slice of fresh pineapple.

2 Keeping the glass upside down, dip the rim into a shallow layer of sugar, coconut or salt. Redip the glass, if necessary, and turn it so that the rim is well-coated.

3 Stand the glass upright and let it sit until the sugar, coconut or salt has dried on the rim, then chill.

Making basic sugar syrup

A sugar syrup is sometimes preferable to dry sugar for sweetening cocktails, since it blends immediately with the other ingredients. This recipe makes about 750ml/1¼ pints.

350g/12oz sugar
600ml/1 pint water

1 Place the sugar in a heavy pan with the water, and heat gently over a low heat. Stir the mixture with a wooden spoon until all of the sugar has dissolved completely.

2 Brush the sides of the pan with a pastry brush dampened in water, to remove any sugar crystals that might cause the syrup to crystallize.

3 Bring to the boil for 3–5 minutes. Skim any scum away and when no more appears, remove the pan from the heat.

4 Cool and pour into clean, dry, airtight bottles. Keep in the refrigerator for up to one month.

Bartending know-how

Homemade sugar syrup is a useful standby ingredient, and cheaper than buying sirop de gomme, which is simply a straight sugar and water syrup in a bottle. It gives a neutral sweetness, and is only used in small doses.

Steeping vodka with fruit

Vodka can be left to steep and absorb the flavours of a wide variety of soft fruits. This recipe makes about 1.2 litres/2 pints.

450g/1lb raspberries, strawberries
* or pineapple*
225g/8oz sugar
1 litre/1¾ pints vodka

1 Put the fruit in a wide-necked jar, and add the sugar.

2 Add the vodka. Cover tightly. Leave in a cool, dark place for a month, shaking gently every week.

3 Strain through clean muslin (cheesecloth) and squeeze out the rest of the liquid from the steeped fruit. Return the flavoured liquor to a clean bottle and seal. Store in a cool, dark place for up to a year.

Steeping vodka with chillies

The process of steeping vodka with other flavouring agents, such as chillies, creates a whole new sensation. This recipe makes about 1 litre/1¾ pints.

25–50g/1–2oz small red chillies, or to taste, washed
1 litre/1³/₄ pints vodka

1 Using a cocktail stick (toothpick), prick the chillies all over to release their flavours.

2 Pack the chillies tightly into a sterilized bottle.

3 Top up with vodka. Fit the cork tightly and leave in a dark place for at least ten days or up to two months.

Making twists

As an alternative to slices of the fruit, drinks can be garnished with a twist of orange, lemon or lime rind. Twists should be made before the drink itself is prepared, so that you don't keep a cold cocktail waiting. Here's how:

1 Choose a citrus fruit with an unblemished skin and a regular shape.

2 Using a canelle knife or potato peeler, start at the tip of the fruit and start peeling round, as though you were peeling an apple.

3 Work slowly and carefully down the fruit, being sure to keep the pared-away rind in one continuous strip.

4 Trim it, if necessary, to a length that suits the glass.

5 A long twist in a cocktail glass makes the drink look sophisticated and elegant, and can be enhanced by the addition of a slice of the same fruit on the rim of the glass.

the cocktails

Screwdriver

The Screwdriver is the original vodka and orange, so named – as the story has it – after an American oil-rig worker developed the habit of stirring his drink with a screwdriver. Presumably, swizzle-sticks are in rather short supply on oil-rigs. As a member of the classic cocktail repertoire, it probably only dates from the 1950s, which is when vodka made its first, tentative appearance on Western markets. The rest is history.

2 measures/3 tbsp vodka
4 measures/6 tbsp orange juice

Add the ingredients, spirit first, to a rocks glass or whisky tumbler loaded with ice cubes, and throw in a slice of orange. Made with freshly squeezed rather than commercial juice, the drink tastes more grown-up and appears to pack more of a punch, as the juice is naturally thinner than concentrate orange juice from a carton.

Moscow Mule

One of the classic American vodka-based cocktails, the Moscow Mule was invented at a Los Angeles restaurant in 1947 as part of the first US sales drive for the Smirnoff brand. It should contain enough vodka to give the drink a real kick, as befits a mule.

2 measures/3 tbsp vodka
¹/₄ measure/1 tsp lime juice
*3 measures/4¹/₂ tbsp sparkling
  ginger ale*

Pour the vodka and lime juice into a highball glass half-filled with ice. Mix together well with a bar spoon. Top up the mixture with ginger ale, and add a few halved slices of lime to the cocktail.

Black Russian

The true Black Russian is simply equal measures of vodka and Tia Maria, or Kahlúa, mixed with ice cubes in a tumbler. However, the fashion in recent years has been to serve it as a long drink in a big glass, topped up with cola.

2 measures/3 tbsp vodka
1 measure/1½ tbsp Tia Maria
   or Kahlúa

Proportions of the classic Black Russian vary according to taste. Two parts vodka to one part Tia Maria on ice, with no mixer, makes a very adult drink.

Certain aficionados insist on Kahlúa rather than Tia Maria with the vodka. Either way, it is as well not to adulterate the drink with cola.

Golden Russian

This is a quite distinct drink from Black or White Russians, in which the vodka acts to take a little of the sweetness off the liqueur, while the lime sharpens it all up still further. It's a very powerful mixture.

1½ measures/6 tsp vodka
1 measure/1½ tbsp Galliano
¼ measure/1 tsp lime juice

Pour all the ingredients into a rocks glass over plenty of cracked ice, and stir. Add a slice of lime.

Bartending know-how
A creamy version of the Black Russian, a White Russian needs shaking rather than stirring, so as to incorporate the cream. Shake 1 measure/1½ tbsp vodka with 1 measure/1½ tbsp Kahlúa or Tia Maria and 1 measure/1½ tbsp whipping cream and ice. Strain into a cocktail glass.

Blenheim

A further twist on the basic Black
Russian idea, the Blenheim uses
orange juice instead of cola, if
you want a non-alcoholic mixer
in there. The resulting colour is
not the loveliest, but the flavour
is better than it sounds.

1¹/₂ measures/6 tsp vodka
³/₄ measure/3 tsp Tia Maria
³/₄ measure/3 tsp orange juice

Shake all the ingredients well with
ice, and strain into a cocktail glass.

Bullshot

The Bullshot is a sort of Bloody Mary, only with beef consommé replacing the tomato juice. It too is thought to have amazing restorative powers as a reviving breakfast drink after the previous night's indulgence. It can be handy if you really can't bear to eat anything, but drink some water first.

2 measures/3 tbsp vodka
4 measures/6 tbsp cold beef
    consommé (classically
    Campbell's)
1/2 measure/2 tsp lemon juice
1/4 measure/1 tsp Worcestershire
    sauce
2 dashes Tabasco
pinch celery salt
pinch cayenne pepper

Mix all the ingredients with ice in a pitcher, and then strain into a highball glass half-filled with ice.

Gipsy

The ingredients in this recipe make for an exotically scented and slightly bittersweet mixture. It would make a highly unusual digestif to enjoy at the end of a grand dinner.

2 measures/3 tbsp vodka
1 measure/1¹/₂ tbsp Bénédictine
dash Angostura bitters

Add the ingredients to a whisky tumbler or Old-Fashioned glass half-full of cracked ice, and stir gently.

Kiss and Tell

A thoroughly exotic mixture of flavours goes into this modern cocktail, and the resulting throbbingly vibrant colour is something to be seen.

1 measure/1¹/₂ tbsp vodka
¹/₂ measure/2 tsp Galliano
¹/₄ measure/1 tsp dry vermouth
¹/₄ measure/1 tsp blue curaçao
2 measures/3 tbsp orange juice
1 measure/1¹/₂ tbsp passion
    fruit juice

Bartending know-how
The blue Bols curaçao is so popular that it is probably now the flagship product of their liqueur range.

Shake all the ingredients with roughly crushed ice and pour everything out into a tall glass. Garnish with a half-slice of orange and a cherry.

Bloody Mary

Everybody has his or her own recipe for the next best hangover cure after aspirin. Some strange people even put tomato ketchup into it. Others round out the alcohol with a splash of dry sherry. Here is my own formula.

5ml/1 tsp Worcestershire sauce
5ml/1 tsp freshly squeezed lemon juice
pinch celery salt
about 6 drops Tabasco
ground black pepper
tomato juice
1 measure/1¹/₂ tbsp vodka

Put a slice of lemon and 2–3 ice cubes in a tall glass, add the first five ingredients, using about six twists of the black pepper mill. Stir to coat the ice. Fill the glass to about 4cm/1¹/₂in from the top with tomato juice and pour in a generous measure of vodka. Stir well.

Dickson's Bloody Mary

This recipe has plenty of spicy character, with horseradish, sherry and Tabasco. Made with chilli or pepper vodka, it is a much hotter proposition than the standard recipe.

2 measures/3 tbsp chilli-flavoured vodka
1 measure/1¹/₂ tbsp fino sherry
7 measures/150ml/¹/₄ pint tomato juice
1 measure/1¹/₂ tbsp lemon juice
2–3 dashes Tabasco
10–15ml/2–3 tsp Worcestershire sauce
2.5ml/¹/₂ tsp creamed horseradish
5ml/1 tsp celery salt
salt and ground black pepper
celery stalk, stuffed green olives and a cherry tomato, to decorate

1 Fill a pitcher with cracked ice and add the vodka, sherry and tomato juice. Stir well. Add the lemon juice, Tabasco, Worcestershire sauce and horseradish. Stir again.

2 Add the celery salt, salt and pepper, and stir until the pitcher has frosted. Strain into a tall tumbler, half-filled with ice. Add the celery and decorate with olives and a cherry tomato.

Cooch Behar

This drink was supposedly created in an idle moment by the Maharajah of that eponymous part of India. It is basically a stripped-down, hot Bloody Mary.

2 measures/3 tbsp chilli or pepper vodka
4 measures/6 tbsp tomato juice

Add the ingredients to a rocks glass or whisky tumbler packed with ice cubes.

Salty Dog

The name refers to the salt frosting that the glass is given. Otherwise, this is a bracingly sour and simple mixture of vodka and grapefruit juice that makes a good aperitif.

5 measures/120ml/4fl oz
grapefruit juice
fine-ground sea salt
2 measures/3 tbsp vodka

Salt the rim of a highball glass by dipping it first in grapefruit juice and then in fine-ground sea salt. Half-fill it with cracked ice. Shake the liquid ingredients together with ice, and then strain into the prepared chilled glass. Add a decorative twist of grapefruit rind.

Soviet Cocktail

This is an American drink intended as a sort of grudging acknowledgement of its old adversary, the USSR.

1½ measures/6 tsp vodka
½ measure/2 tsp dry vermouuth
½ measure/2 tsp medium-dry
(amontillado) sherry

Shake all the ingredients well with ice, and strain into a cocktail glass. Squeeze a twist of lemon rind over the top and drop it into the drink.